The KiDS' Book of Things That GO

By
Lisa Haughom

kidsbooks
Incorporated

On the Road

Off the Road

In the City

bus

street cleaner

horse and buggy

garbage truck

motorcycle

ambulance

mounted police officer

bicycle

stroller

subway

On the Farm

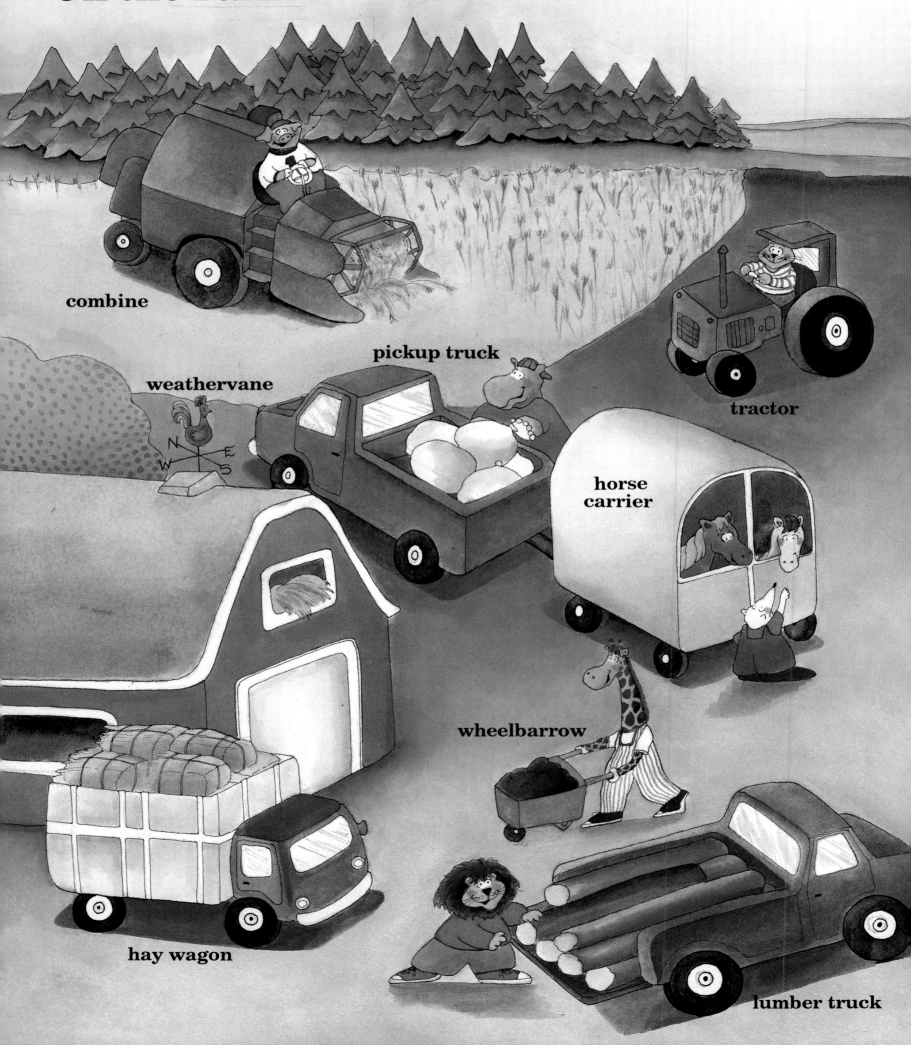

combine

weathervane

pickup truck

tractor

horse
carrier

wheelbarrow

hay wagon

lumber truck

grass
cutter

windmill

riding
lawn mower

produce
truck

buggy

In the Water

sailboat

ocean liner

seaplane

submarine

rowboat

ferry

fishing boat

police boat

At the Amusement Park

roller coaster

ferris wheel

log flume

train ride

boat ride

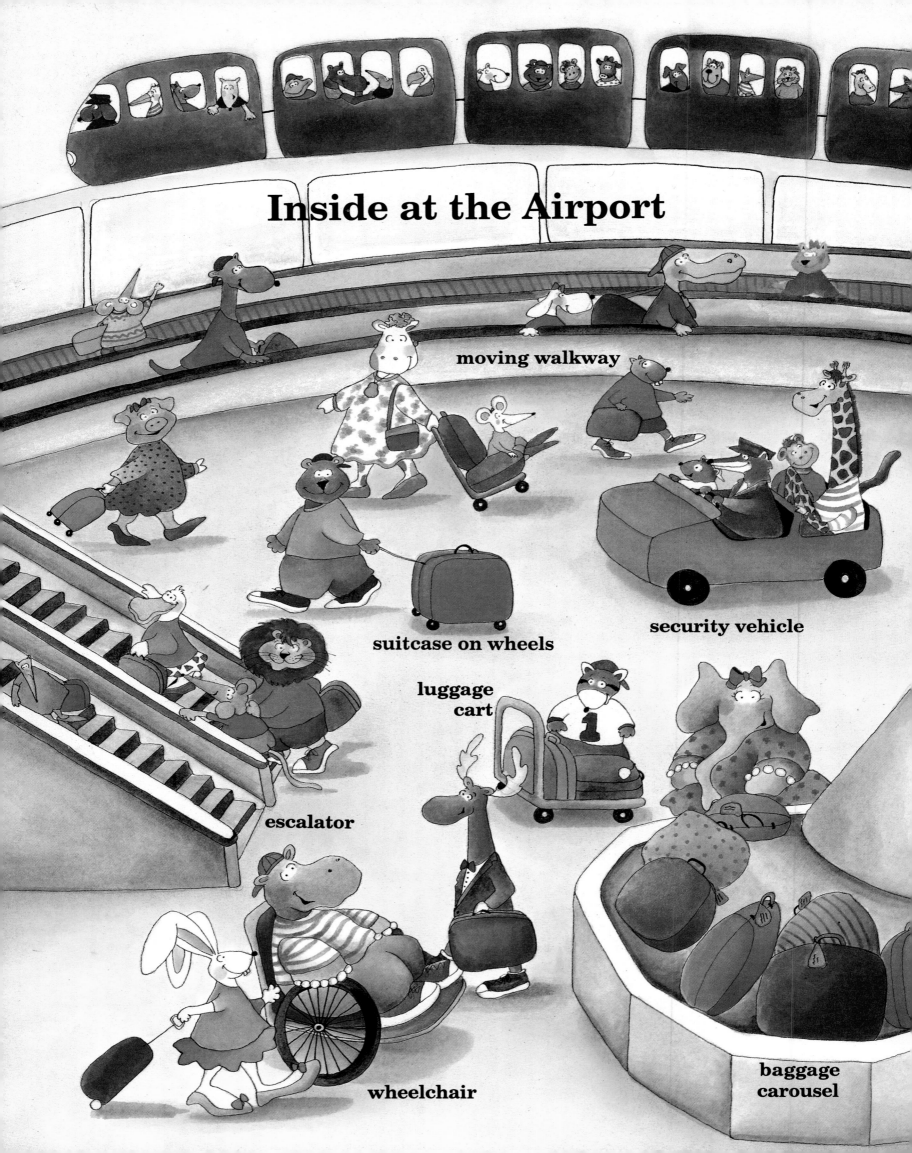

Inside at the Airport

moving walkway

suitcase on wheels

security vehicle

luggage cart

escalator

wheelchair

baggage carousel

Outside at the Airport

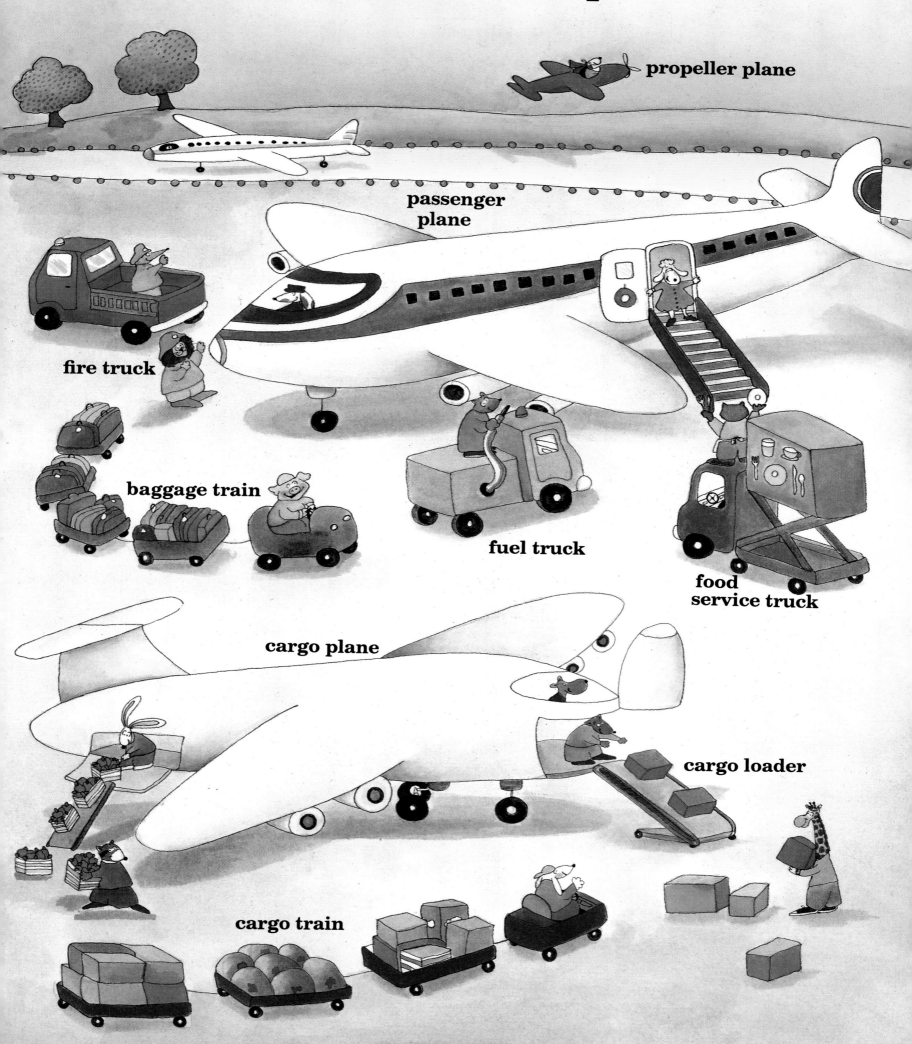

propeller plane

passenger plane

fire truck

baggage train

fuel truck

food service truck

cargo plane

cargo loader

cargo train

space shuttle

blimp

private jet

fighter plane

hot air balloon

hang glider

In the Air

passenger plane

satellite

propeller plane

military plane

parachute

ultralight

helicopter

ditch digger

cherry picker

cement mixer

scoop loader

bulldozer

power roller

dump truck

At Work

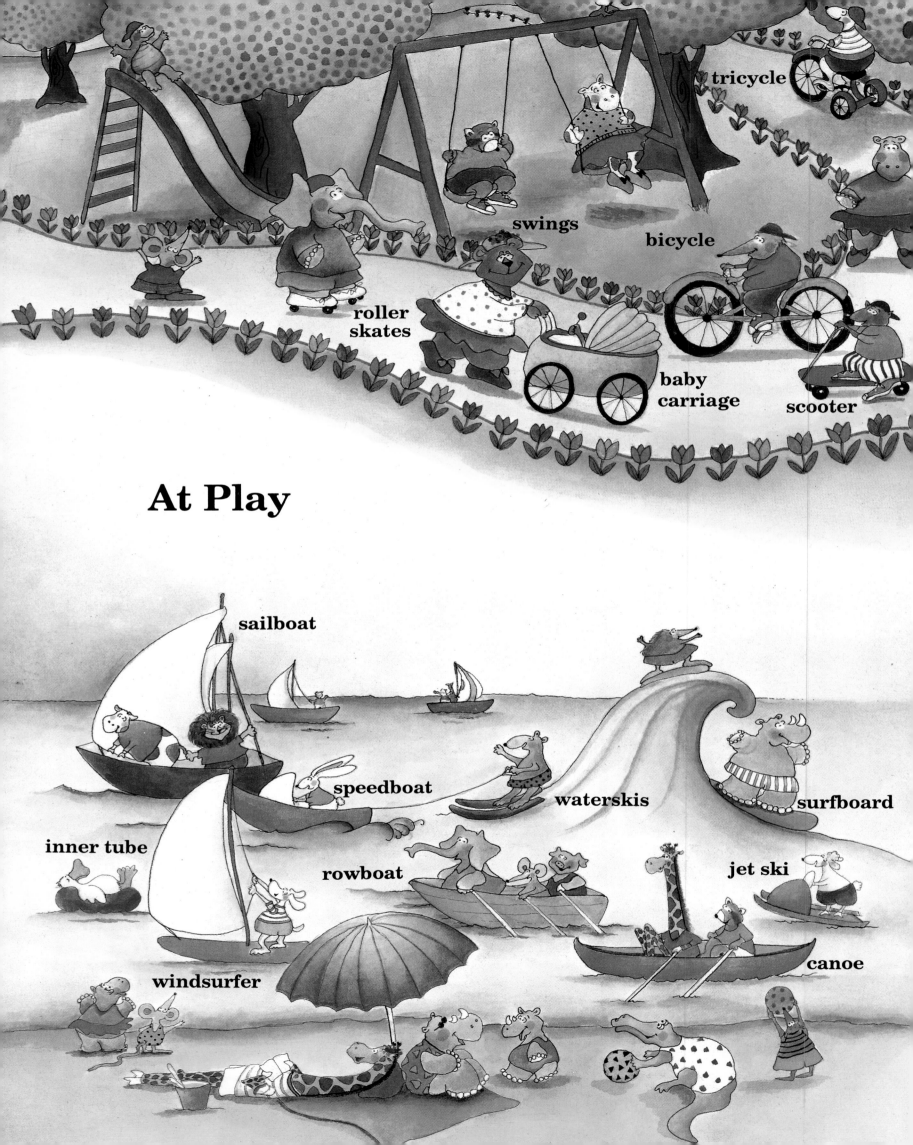

tricycle

swings

bicycle

roller
skates

baby
carriage

scooter

At Play

sailboat

speedboat

waterskis

surfboard

inner tube

rowboat

jet ski

windsurfer

canoe

kite

two-seater bicycle

skateboard

wagon

in-line skates

skis

chair lift

toboggan

sled

snowboard

snowmobile

sleigh

ice skates

Around Town

lawn mower

family car

school bus

motor scooter

ice-cream truck

jeep

trailer home

hose on wheels

station wagon

bicycle

mail truck

mobile home

4x4 recreational vehicle

baby carriage

minivan

riding lawn mower

At the Toy Store

balls

pogo sticks

push toy

toy truck

toy car

wagon

toy train

wooden soldiers

baby walker

pull toy

toy boats

toy airplane

kiddie car

roller skates

tops

doll carriage

in-line skates

rocking horse

remote control car